Karrie Ross

IMPACT OF
LIFE

August 2014

LA Artcore Union Center for the Arts

Impact of Life
by Karrie Ross

Copyright © 2014 Karrie Ross

Karrie Ross
12516 Washington Place, Los Angeles, CA 90066
Visit our website at www.KarrieRoss.com.

Printed in the United States of America

Book Design by Be It Now! Karrie Ross

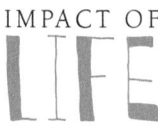

IMPACT OF LIFE

"Impact of LIFE" spans a variety of images offering surreal faces, and the light/dark whimsy of a figure with an egg, to her exploration of impact craters form and energy transference. Her questions arise from social, scientific, and internal personal investigations.

The exhibition features a selection of ink & paint pieces from Ross' most recent work and sets to recount her whimsical view of living through difficult situations over the past two-years time. *"It, the exploration of the ink & paint style and process, has finally come together for me. The imagery is not only fun, compelling and balances my energetic needs, it brings my essence in touch with what is going on in my life in a safe way, so I can better relate to it. The ink satisfies my never-ending need to be active, to 'take' me out of the now into a flowing space in mind, mixed with the painting aspect, providing a safe seamless connection."*

There are three series represented.

I Am The Egg! follows the expressive figures of a man and a woman as they interact within the egg world. The egg representing the sensitivity and delicateness of the eggshell, and how it stays strong through play and whimsy, in the world of question.

Energy Impact Crater explores the makings of our universe, the force that created it, as well as the continuing vibration and energy dispersement that exists because of it… the Big Bang creation.

Surreal presenting the seeing of thoughts and items in juxtaposition of each other, being logical or not… existing in a moment of the illusive illusion of time and space inviting you into the not-here.

Karrie's work centers around the personal generation of a continuous flow of energy and her belief that this energy can be shared with the world through exploring art, haikus, writing, and exampling the concepts of feng shui energy balancing.

Karrie is a native of Los Angeles and describes herself as visual artist who creates art with abandon.

Karrie Ross : LA Artcore Union Center for the Arts 2014

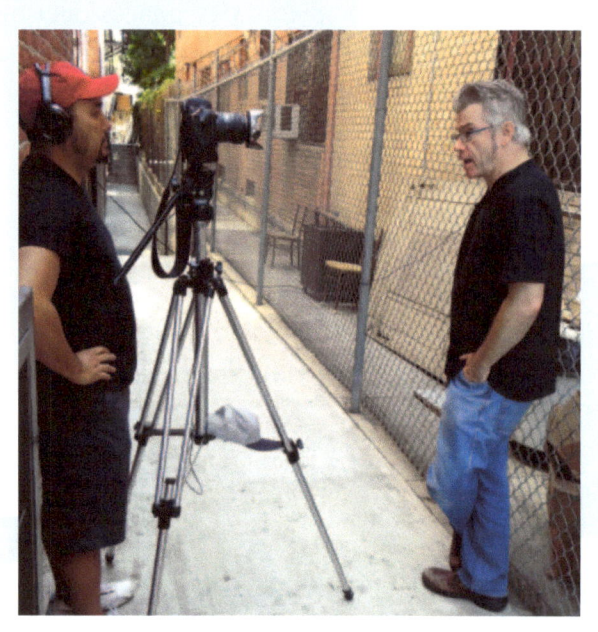

"When you are looking at drawings you are looking at rough drafts for what a painting can be. A very linear planned and structured, few erasure marks to get things precise. The most interesting drawing, and drawing as a medium is an art form, for me, is when I'm looking at it as a viewer is improvisational drawing. Karrie Ross takes that to an even more intense level by starting with and incorporating accidents throughout her process.

And so when you let literally fate and physics conspire, the level of freedom in that and the level of confidence of an artist is — A. it's rare, and B. that she pulls it off that she makes these compelling drawings that are as structured as any preplanned notion. What's special about them for me, is that they're almost finished paintings and yet they are still drawings so that there's that energy of the what-might-happen with the insistence though that this is a painting that's 'going to live on for generations—this object that's going to carry today forever...'"

~**Mat Gleason**; writer, curator, dealer (transcribed from the show video)

"A Catalyst of Meaning: The Art of Karrie Ross"

by Jill Thayer, Ph.D.

For centuries, artists have explored the conceptual boundaries of art and science, such as Da Vinci, whose empirical methodologies revealed the creative discoveries of imagination and curiosity. Those mechanisms of gestalt inspired many in the notions of visual perception and, the reality of being. The psychological phenomena that occurred throughout the process would open the door for wonderers to come. Karrie Ross is an artist who sees the realms of existence through a multi-faceted lens: energy, science, participation, conversations, and being seen are influencing constructs of her work. She notes that, "metaphorical representations create a 'safe' place for the viewer to experience a flow and connection from their interaction with the art, discovering that they are part of a bigger whole." This intent engages a reflexivity between viewer and artist, as Ross defines her process of discovery as one that is intertwined with learning about matter itself, such as the molecular vibrations of an atom that require energy in transitions—and that everything has a frequency, which the universe reciprocates. She adds, "I paint with abandon, and my belief system is that we're all connected through the vibrational energy of the earth that is natural."

Change is a catalyst in her work. Ross acknowledges that it can be a simple "Aha" moment and cites that change is in the magic created within the mystery of living life— a paradigm shift.

"I change moment-by-moment. My life is an illusion that I create. My 'what is' is right now. I don't paint based on what's happening in the world. I paint what is happening within me in reaction to what's happening in the world. A context is formed from what my subconscious needs me to expose so the art changes a

perspective into a response. I have no idea what that is until the art is finished. Balanced. I start with a symbol or figure but all the rest just happens when one is put next to another over and over again."

Watercolor is the primary media that Ross uses. The painting begins on a dry palette with infusions of pen and ink, oil and acrylic, and sometimes torn paper. Her doodles are reminiscent of Cy Twombly's organic scribbles set in a field of lyrical abstraction. Spirals, a tonality of blended color, and metallic bejeweling embellish a framework that is grounded in graphic design and color theory. Stylized figures appear whimsical yet allegorical in a resplendent cavalcade to ignite the viewer's attention.

The juxtaposition of semiotic imagery and magical realism creates a *mise-en-scène* that is metaphoric of Brecht's theatrical alienation, in which the audience is distanced from emotional involvement by a simulated performance. Figurative and graphic illustrations are cast as playful characters that dance across each piece with quizzical abandon. These incarnations seem to veil an angst that serves as a touchstone and catharsis for Ross, perhaps for life's complexities. Yet ultimately, these sub-layers of existence reveal her luminous characters in a joyful expression of synergistic continuum.

IMPACT OF

LIFE

IMAGES THAT WERE IN THE SHOW:

I AM THE EGG! LADY #1

I AM THE EGG! MAN #2

I AM THE EGG! MAN #3

BEJEWELED FISH

TOUCHING

WATCHING THE PODs

ENERGY IMPACT CRATER #1

ENERGY IMPACT CRATER: CHAOTIC BURST

HAND STORY

PARTY CLASS TIME

(THERE ARE OTHER PIECES OF ART ADDED TO THE CATALOG TO
EXAMPLE HOW EACH SERIES EXTENDS OUT)

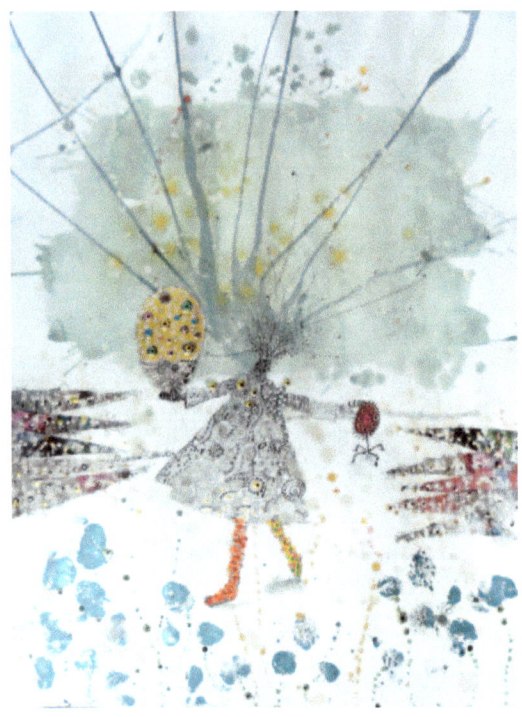

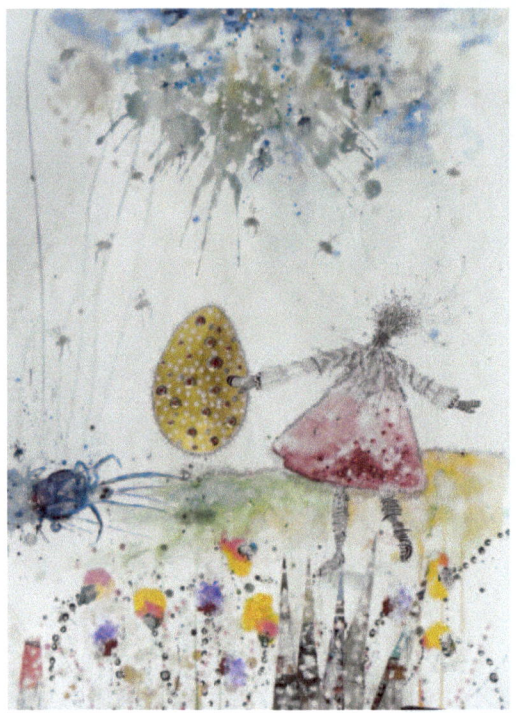

Title: I Am The Egg! Lady #2
Size: 30" x 22"
Medium: oil, acrylic, ink, watercolor,
collage, on arches
Date: 2014

Title: I Am The Egg! Lady #3
Size: 30" x 22"
Medium: oil, acrylic, ink, watercolor, collage on
arches
Date: 2014

Robert Seitz, LA Artcore

Karrie Ross lives a fully creative life, moving daily between two modes of working. As a book designer and author, with a background in advertising and marketing, she creates direct interpretations to suit the assignments she receives. As an artist with fifty years of experience with a full range of mediums, she comfortably shifts to the opposite, and works from instinct and mystery as a way to further the intense focal energy she carries within her.

Her art work is about the pursuit of answerable questions. She lives for them, and frames a life through the use of questions, rules and parameters. Quite different from rules of authority where one is left only to choose obedience or rebellion, the sort of rules she discusses are more like tinkering with the instructions for playing a game. Rules introduced to increase the level of intrigue, parlay with chance, and

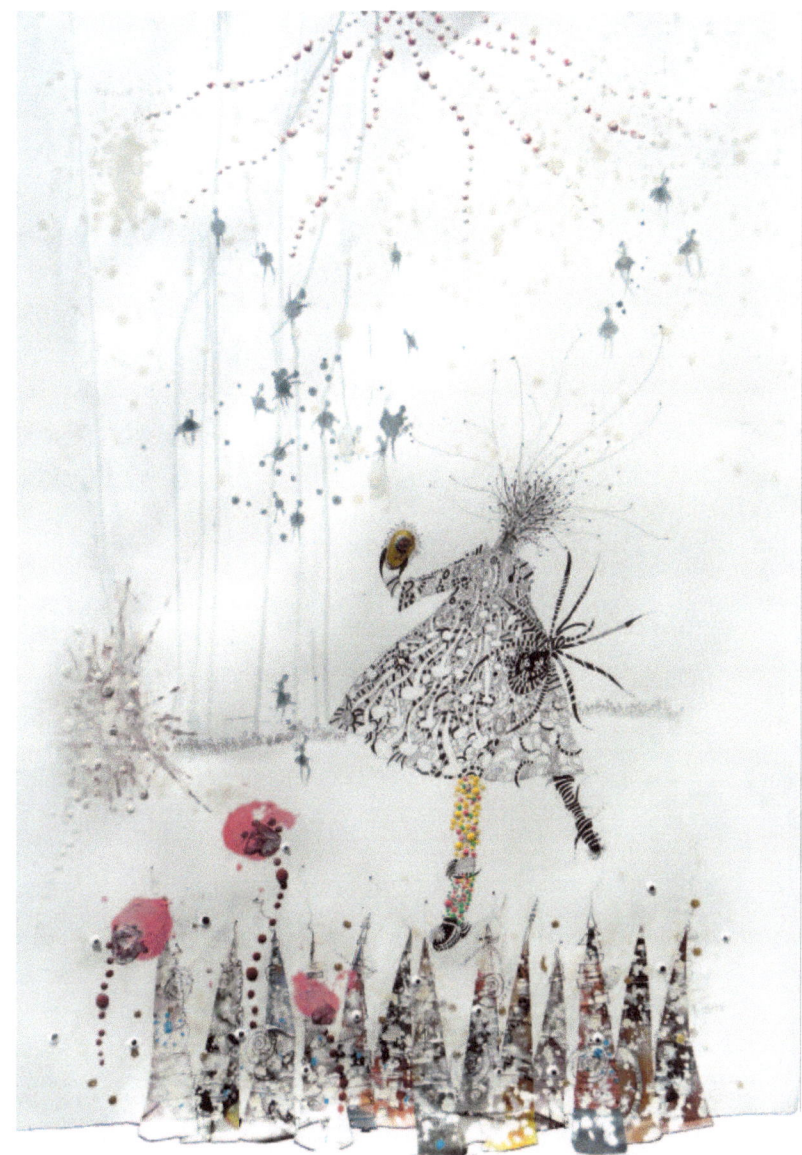

Title: I Am The Egg! Lady #1
Size: 30" x 22"
Medium: oil, acrylic, ink, watercolor, collage, on arches
Date: 2014

Karrie Ross : LA Artcore Union Center for the Arts 2014

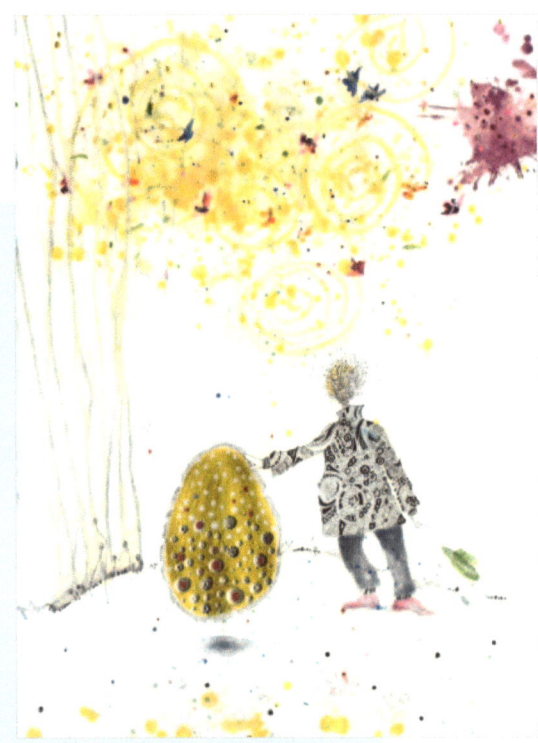

Title: I Am The Egg! Man #1
Size: 30" x 22"
Medium: oil, acrylic, ink, watercolor on arches
Date: 2013

turn a straight line into a garden path. Likewise there isn't an absolute answer so much as call and response, diving and resurfacing beneath the waters of her search in a game of Marco Polo. She searches for an unguided answer in the work, whether it's conscious or unconscious, and uses this to measure the degree of finish in a piece. She moves through materials and surfaces at will, and tends to take on a cluster or group of materials to work over at one time. It is as though she were an irrigation system, trying out new crops in various fields, and directing the gates of her waters in pulses that reach several ends at once.

Creating rules as she works, in the most playful sense, are key to her process. This is significant to her, she wasn't aware of the rules (her own role in making them) when she was younger. Being aware of them means being able to manipulate them, having control over who she is, a source of growth and joy for her as she becomes increasingly familiar with how much she can direct her own perceptions.

The works have a dreamy excess to them, colors outlined with frenetic ink strokes that fizz and pop, her elements in a halo of static electricity. A visiting art critic called these marks obsessive, and in art obsession is not a liability. Spotting the grief in a particular work, Ross was delighted to hear it. Even though there is a pleasant sturdiness, a kind of holistic whimsy that characterizes their outer glow, the devil is in the details, and the pictures are raucous records of many emotions and thoughts. The artist has in reserve specific information regarding what she was going through in a particular piece, but she's not telling, expressing the sentiment of many artists, that she's just not interested in telling others how to see.

In the culture of art there is a prevailing interest in favoring youth. Besides the obvious paradox in reducing the visibility of skill and experience, one misses the examples of possible directions the relationship with one's self can take. Each decade has produced leaps forward for Ross, with the current vocabulary in her work feeling as though it is just a few years old. Beyond the arch claim behind a steady incline of experience, these periodic shifts are a kind of renewal. Each time, meeting herself as a new friend, creates room for new intimacy and understanding. (end RS)

http://www.laartcore.org/Webzine/2014/08/13/karrie-ross/

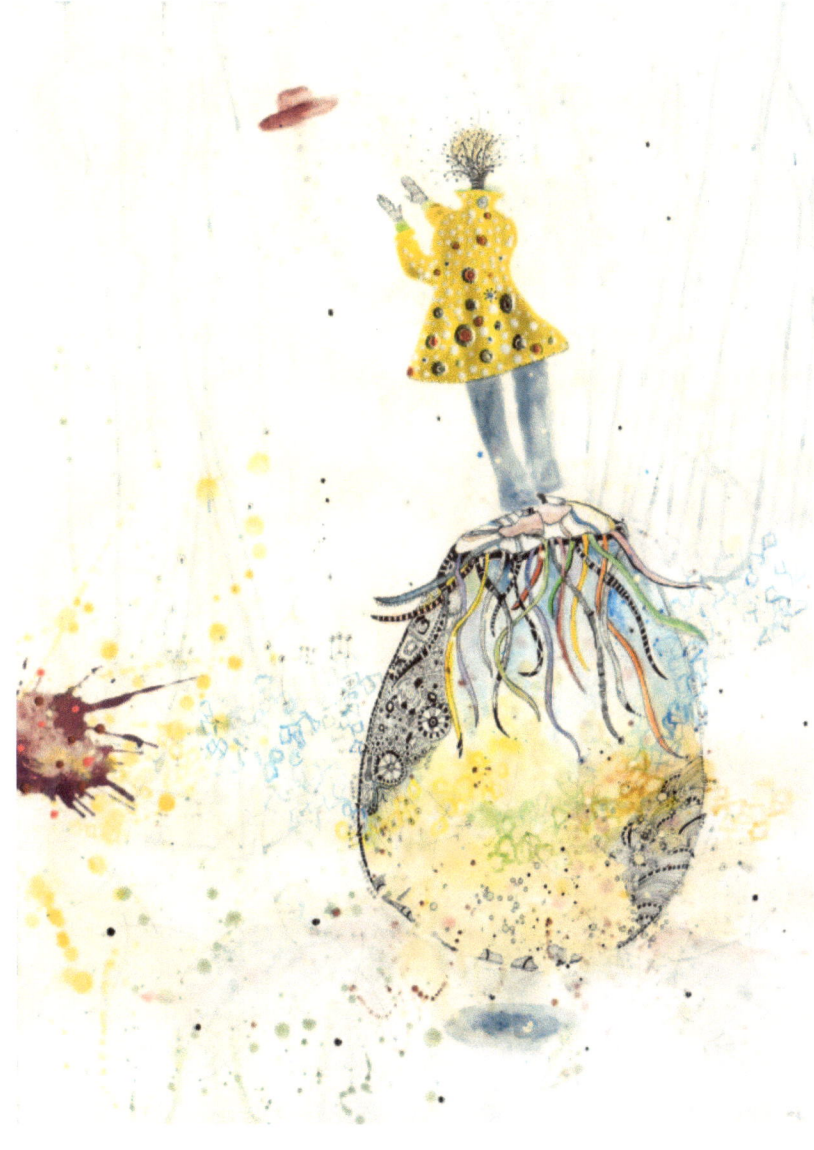

Title: I Am The Egg! Man #2
Size: 30" x 22"
Medium: oil, acrylic, ink, watercolor on arches
Date: 2014

Shana Nys Dambrot, Art Critic, Writer, Curate
(transcribed from the show video)

The only reason I wanted to stop and look at
this particular piece is because I feel it has
elements of all of the different things that
I love, that are going on in other pieces
throughout the whole show, but they've all
found their way into this one image.

What I mean by that is, for example, Karrie
and I have been talking about this abstract
figurative continuum. One of the things I love
about a lot of the work is that, even though it
all very clearly read as a pictorial space with
objects and figures and actions, this piece, if
you take out these seven little trees right there
and you don't see them, this whole expanse
doesn't even necessarily read as a horizon line
anymore.

It reads as this very beautiful gestural...and this
more forceful, and four to five different kinds
of abstraction or abstract expressionism. Then
you put these tiny, little marks a little ink, very
little it couldn't be more schematic. as far as
describing a tree goes. There are a couple of
them, and that's it. Then, all of a sudden, this
whole thing becomes a
horizon line or a hill top.

You have this green color you read as a meadow or a grass or an natural space. You have all this stuff starting to read as a sky, weather, or atmosphere. You get this pictorial space, and all of a sudden, this egg form, it could very easily be a boulder. But you know, if you look throughout the work, that eggs are recurring imagery in the work.

All of the drawing that happens inside of it no longer takes away from it being this object that this figure is standing on. It reads clearly, "I know that there's a lot of accidental brilliance that happened in here, and a few discoveries and things that were worked at and worked at, and then it looks simple and intuitive."

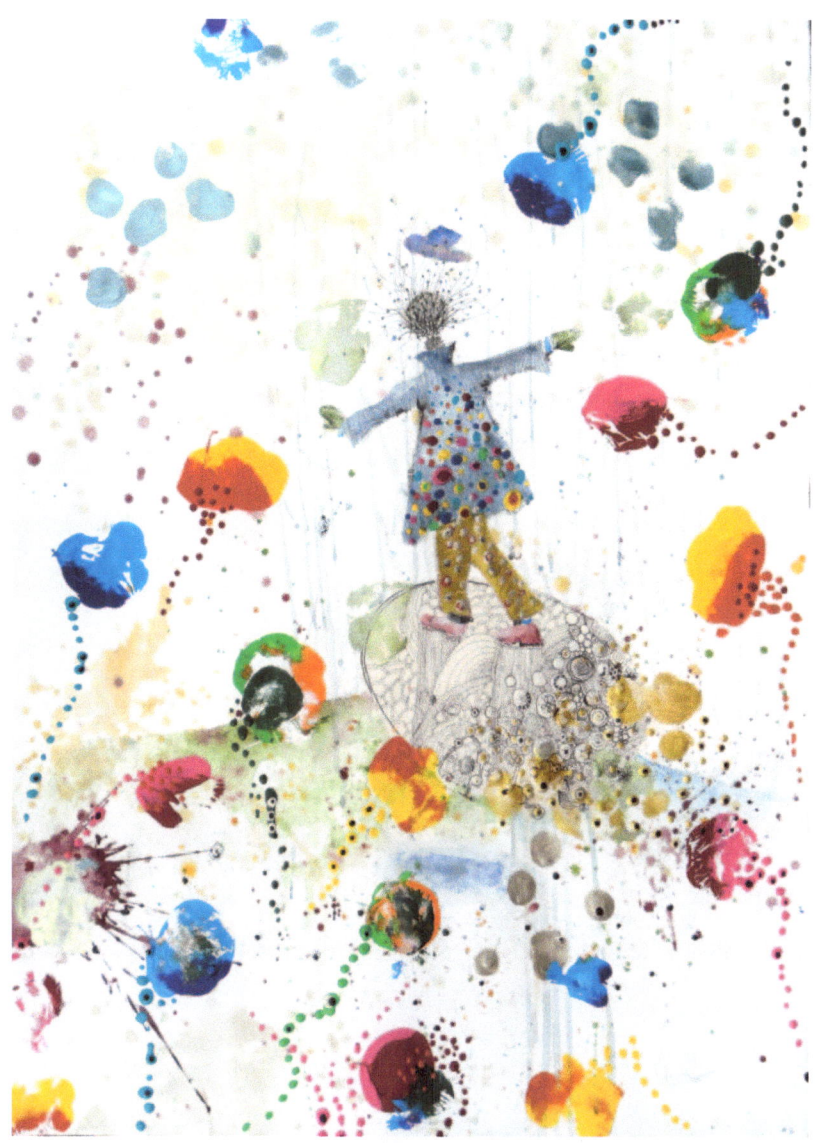

Title: I Am The Egg!   Man #3
Size: 30" x 22"
Medium: oil, acrylic, ink, watercolor on arches
Date: 2014

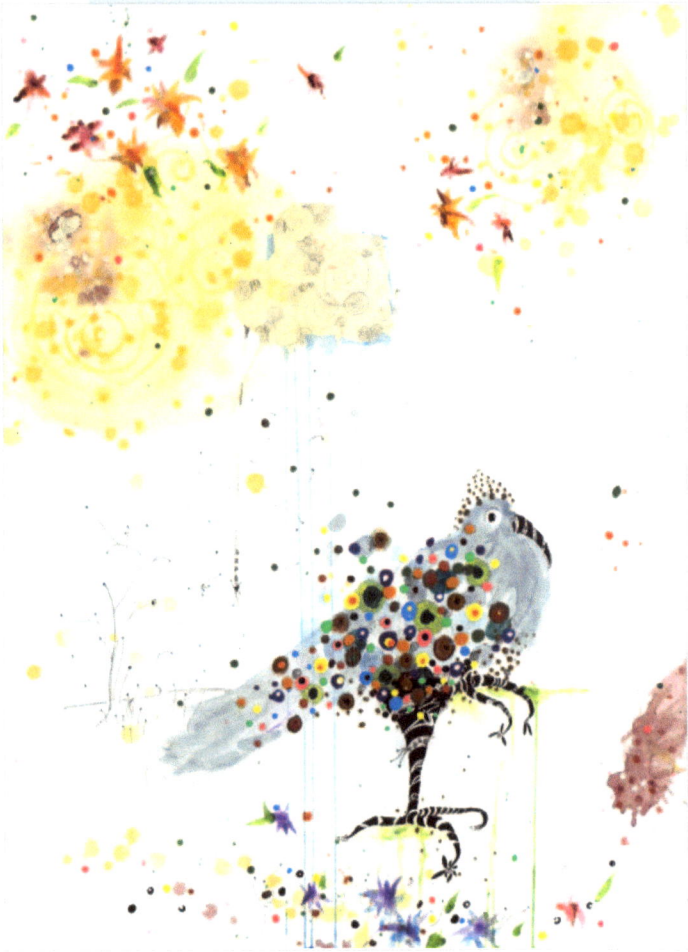

Title: As the Cloud Weeps. Bejeweled Bird (surreal)
Size: 30" x 22"
Medium: oil, acrylic, ink, watercolor on arches
Date: 2013

Shana: I love this fish mostly because, if you take out just its head you don't even have to take out the whole fish, take just head out all of a sudden, the whole thing becomes completely abstract, completely non representational. It becomes about the shapes, the colors, the textures, the tiny, tiny little mark making that's super controlled, the splatters that are much less controlled, and those organic versus ritualistic shapes.

It takes on a completely different character, once you see the whole creature.
Abstract. Fish allegory. All of a sudden, there's narrative "What does that mean? Where does that come from?" and the symbolism that goes on in that.

Video can be seen at:
http://www.karrierossfineart.com/photos/

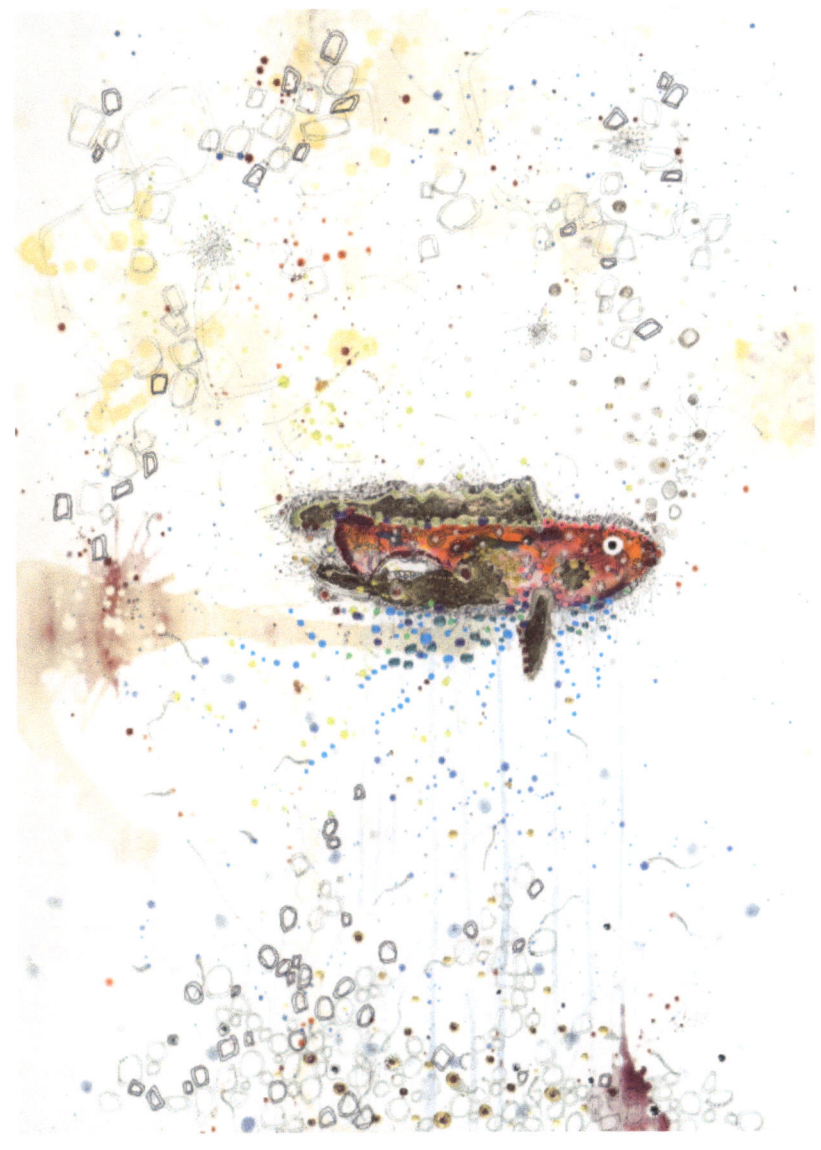

Title: Bejeweled Fish
Size: 30" x 22"
Medium: oil, acrylic, ink, watercolor, gold leaf, on arches
Date: 2013

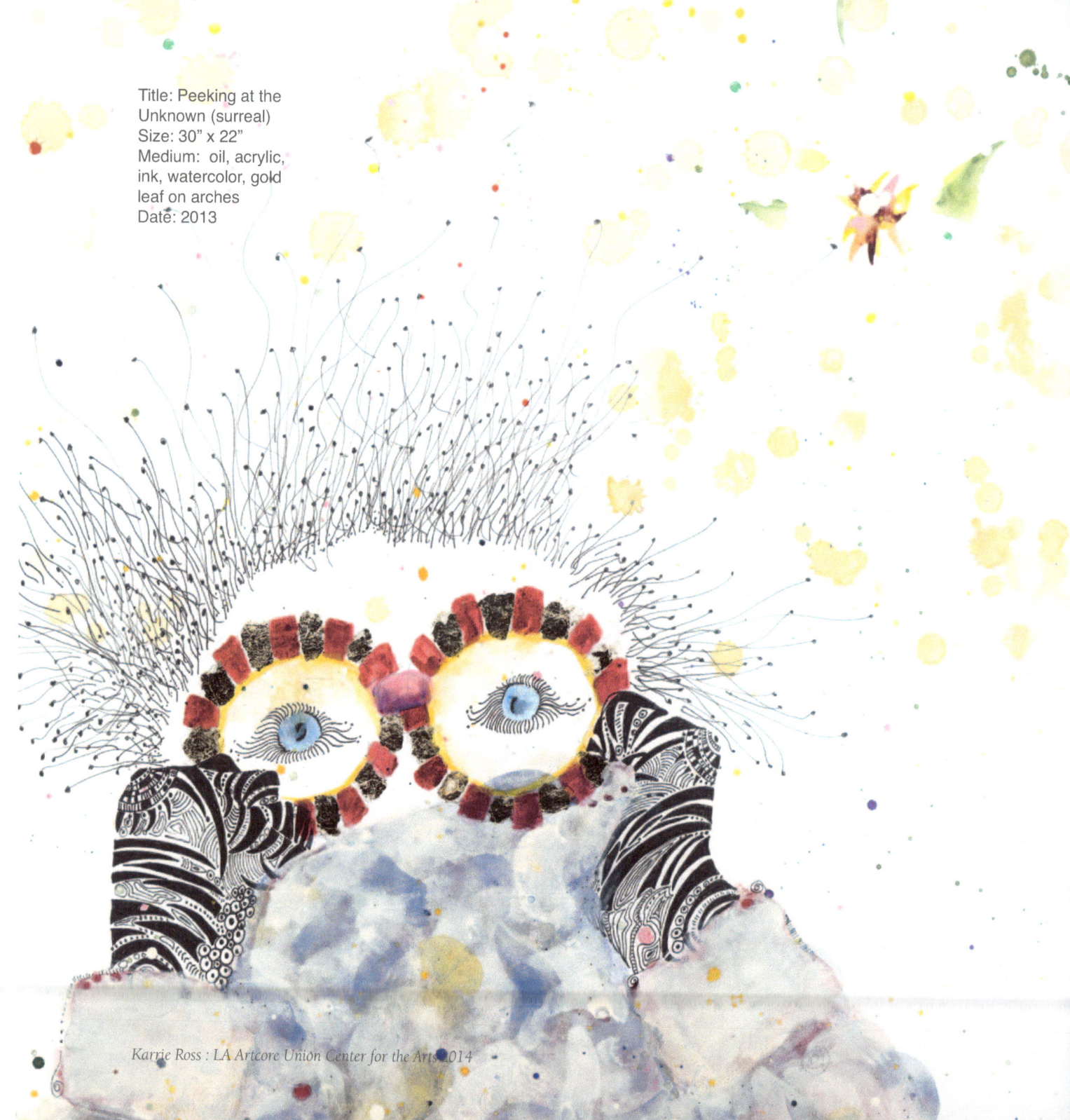

Title: Peeking at the Unknown (surreal)
Size: 30" x 22"
Medium: oil, acrylic, ink, watercolor, gold leaf on arches
Date: 2013

Karrie Ross : LA Artcore Union Center for the Arts 2014

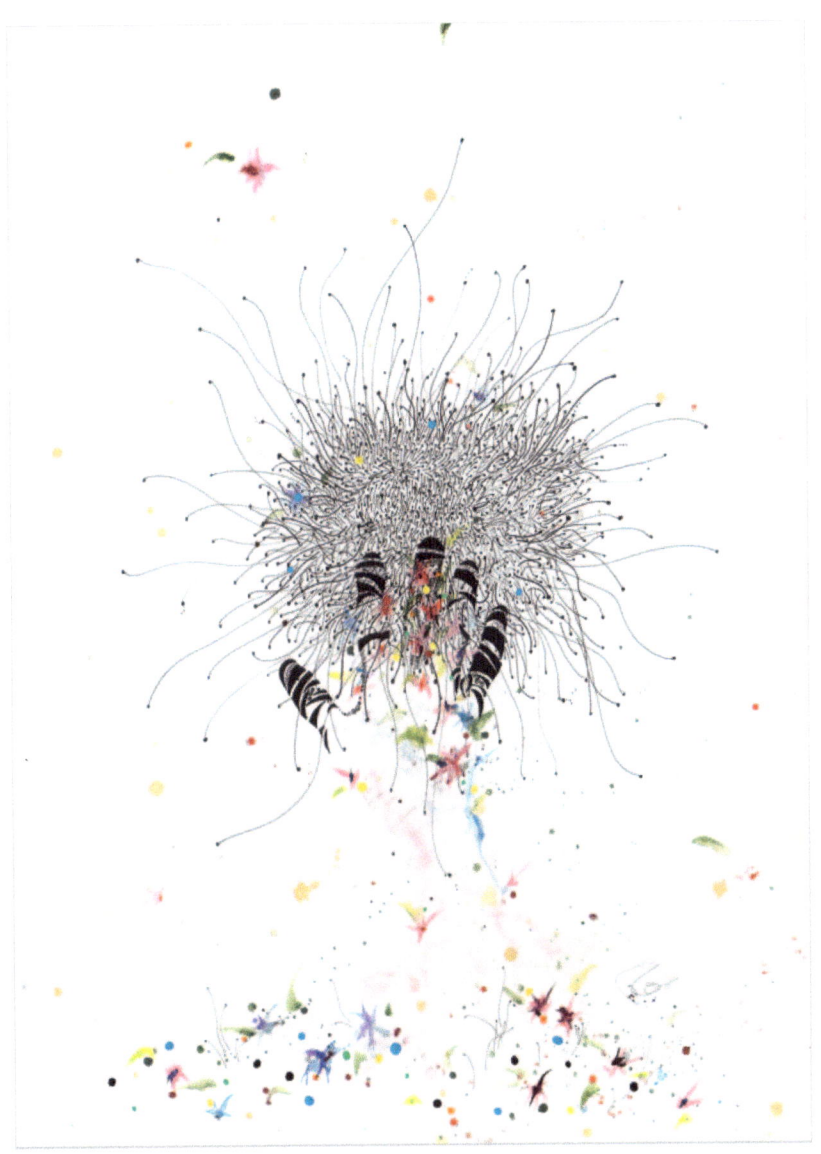

Title: Touching (surreal)
Size: 30" x 22"
Medium: oil, acrylic, ink, watercolor on arches
Date: 2013

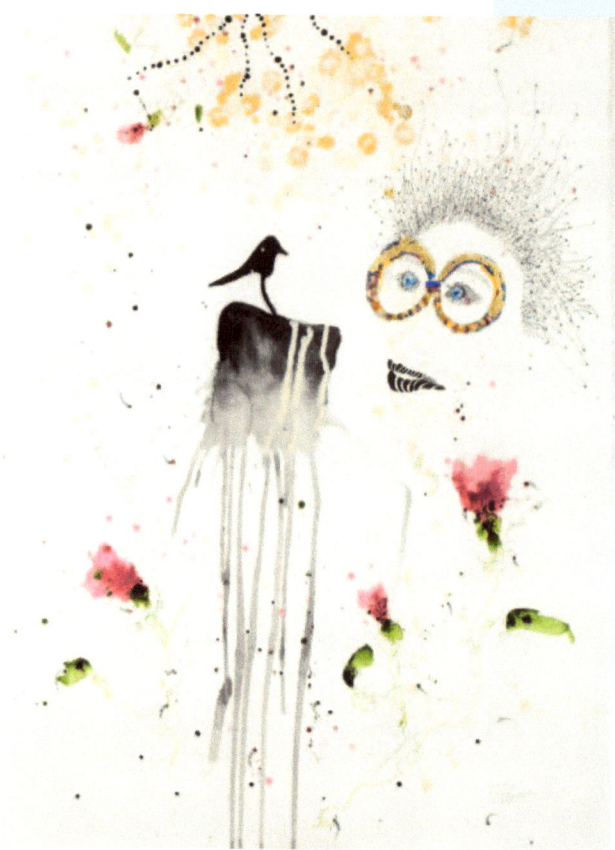

Title: Conversations With Ms. Einstein (surreal)
Size: 30" x 22"
Medium: oil, acrylic, ink, watercolor, gold leaf on arches
Date: 2013

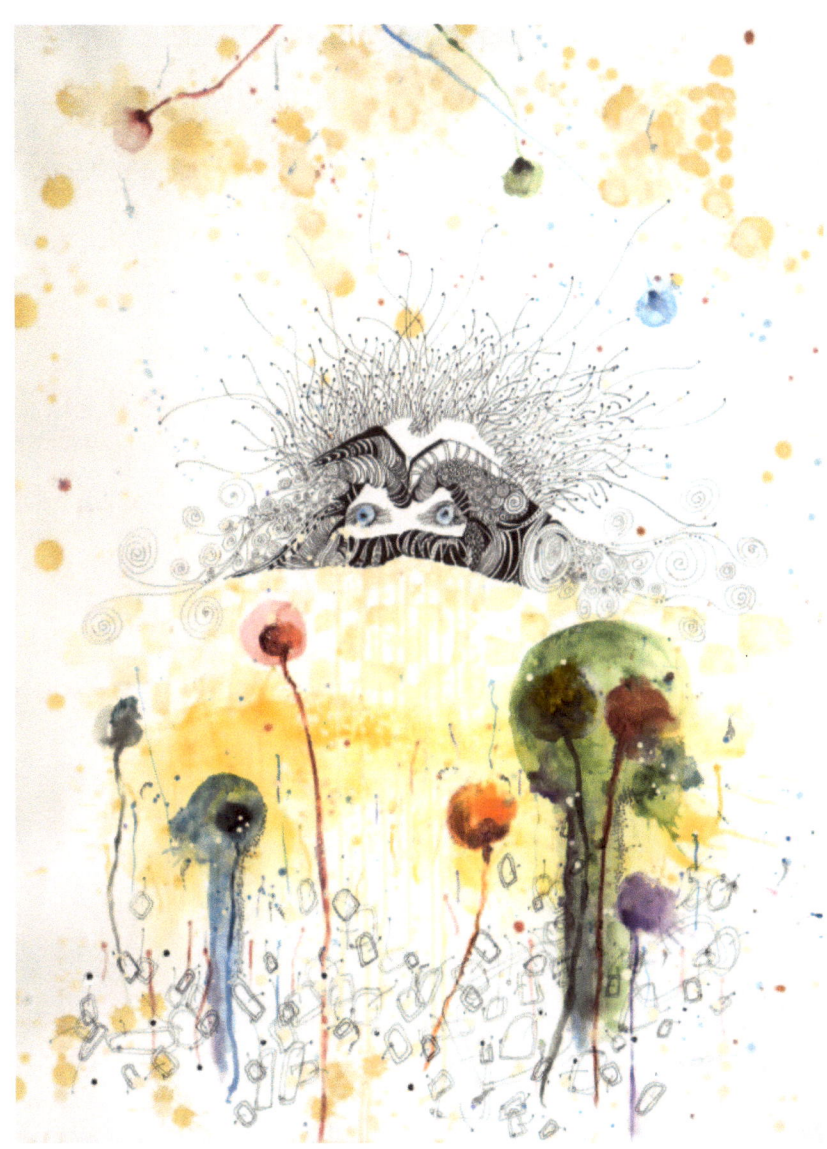

Title: Watching the PODs
Size: 30" x 22"
Medium: oil, acrylic, ink, watercolor on arches
Date: 2013

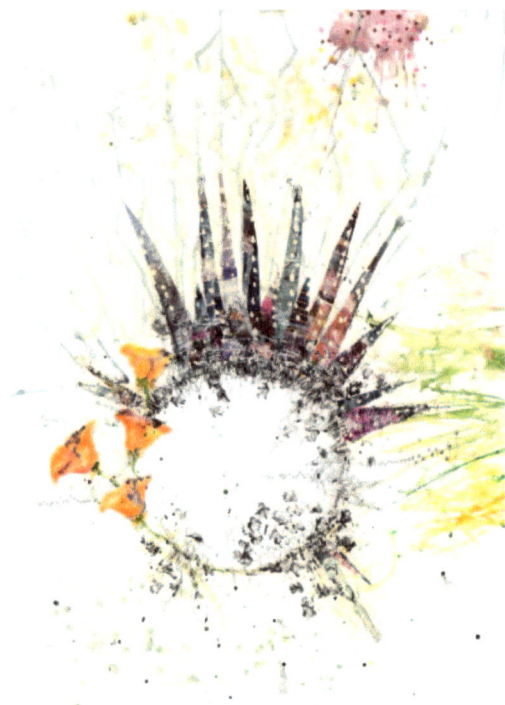

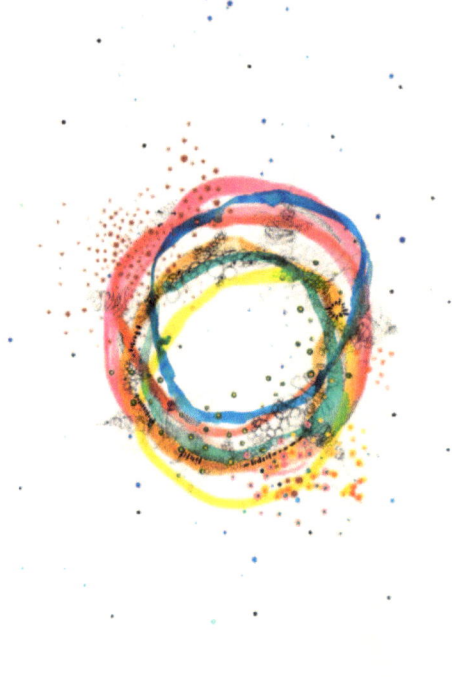

Title: Energy Impact Crater: California
Poppies!
Size: 30" x 22"
Medium: oil, acrylic, ink, watercolor,
collage, on arches
Date: 2014

Title: Energy Impact Cratrer #8
Size: 30" x 22"
Medium: acrylic, ink on arches
Date: 2014

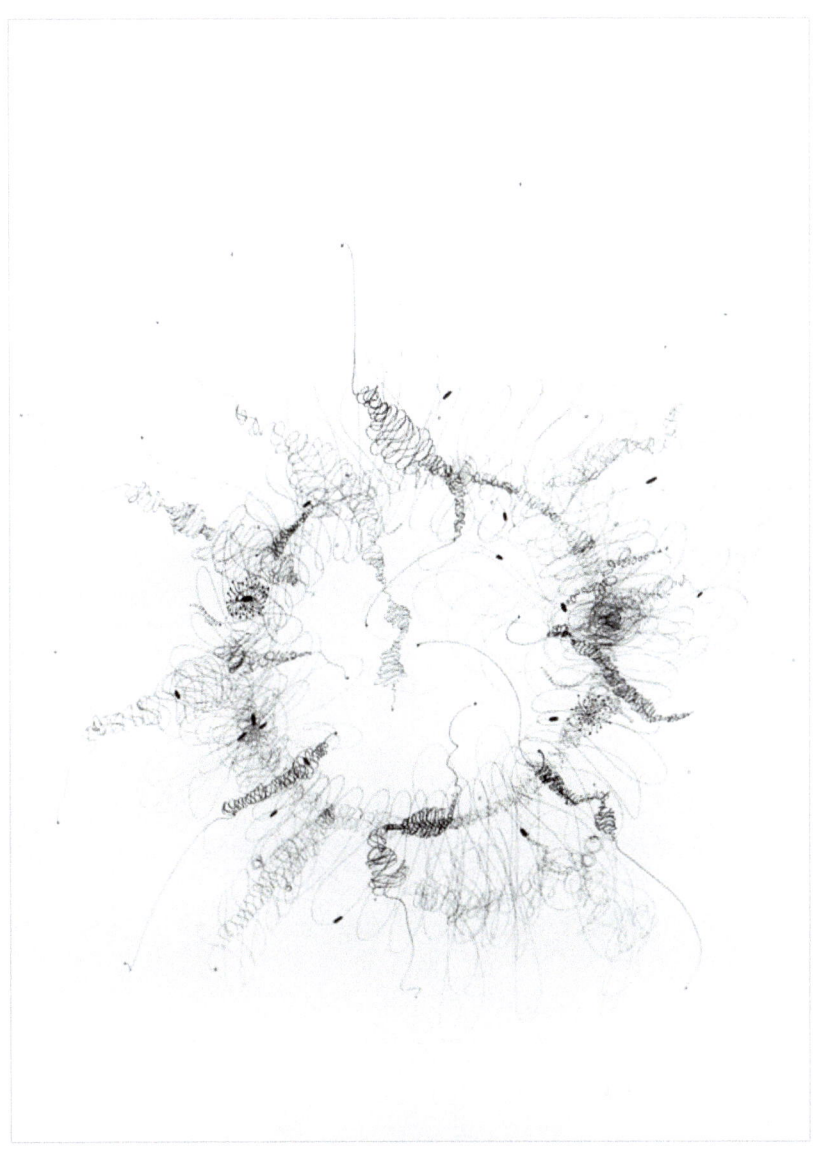

Title: Energy Impact Crater #1
Size: 30" x 22"
Medium: ink on arches
Date: 2013

Karrie Ross : LA Artcore Union Center for the Arts 2014

Title: Energy Impact Crater #5
Size: 30" x 22"
Medium: oil, ink, on arches
Date: 2013

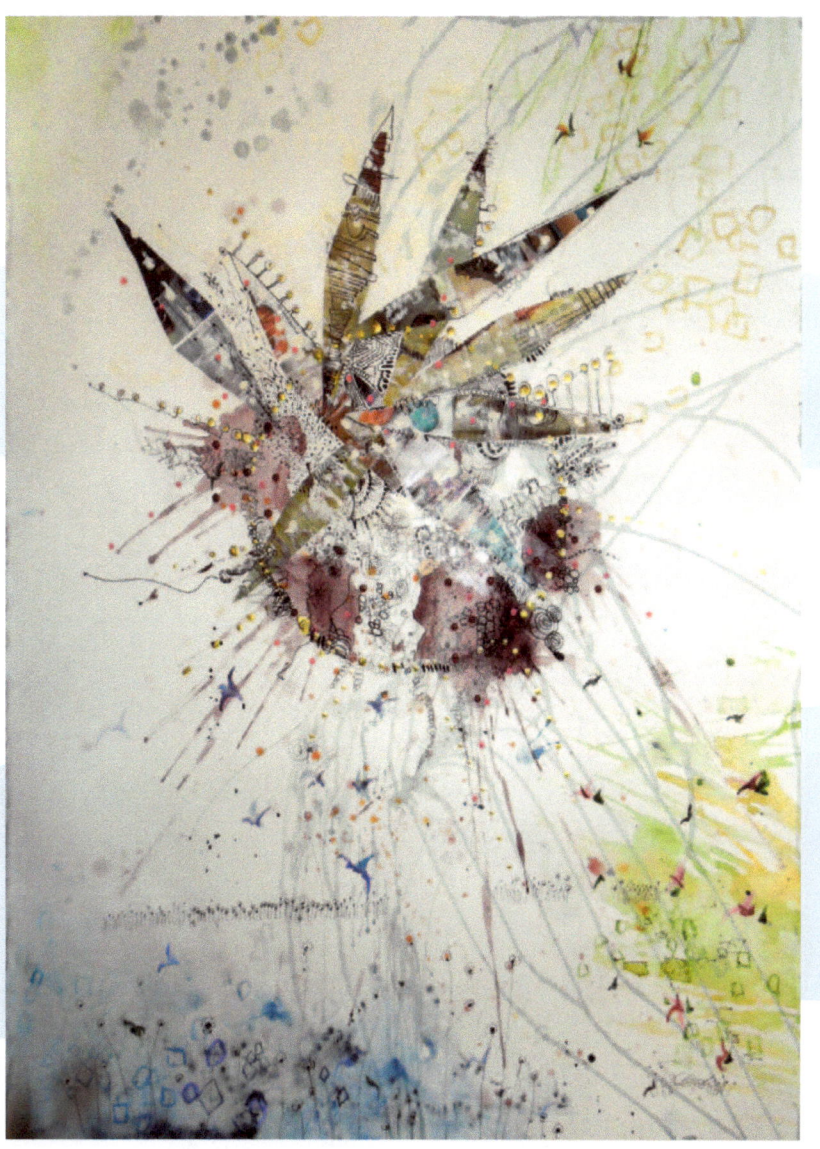

Title: Energy Impact Crater: Chaotic Burst!
Size: 30" x 22"
Medium: oil, acrylic, ink, watercolor on arches
Date: 2014

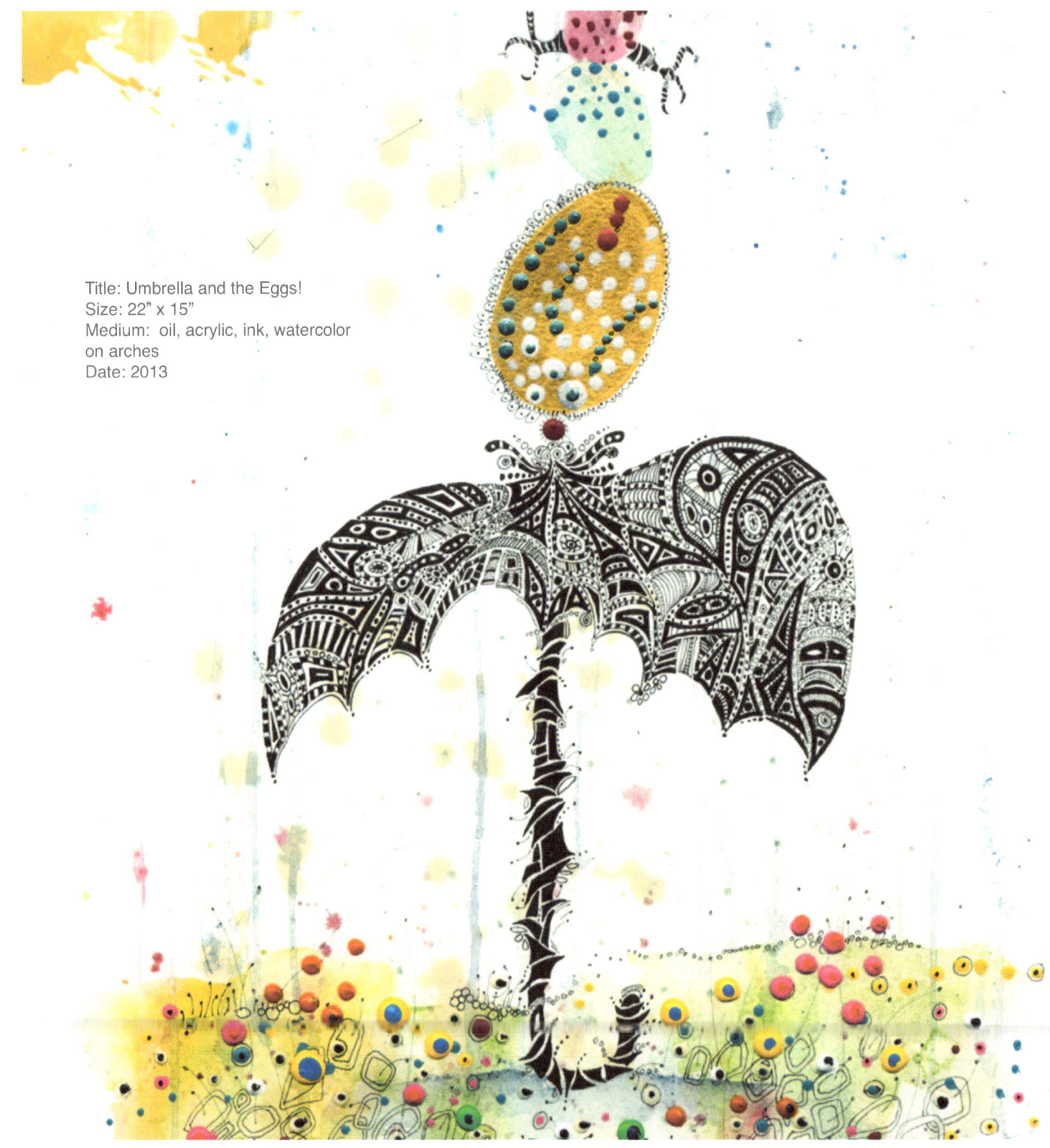

Title: Umbrella and the Eggs!
Size: 22" x 15"
Medium: oil, acrylic, ink, watercolor
on arches
Date: 2013

Shana: This work might be my favorite in the show, partly because the patient, folksy, ritual, decorative density of the way this hand is built is compelling as a matter of drawing, not only because it's a hand, which goes back to the artist and the maker idea, but also because of how clearly, made by hand, one tiny stroke at a time this is.

It highlights the beauty and the obsessive nature of the way that Karrie draws when she draws. But when you get into the works, you start to notice the palette is tertiary, the washes are emotional.

Again, if you imagine yourself making these kinds of marks, at that scale and with that density, that kind of experience is very fraught, psychologically. There's an interesting paradox that happens between the way it looks and the way it feels.

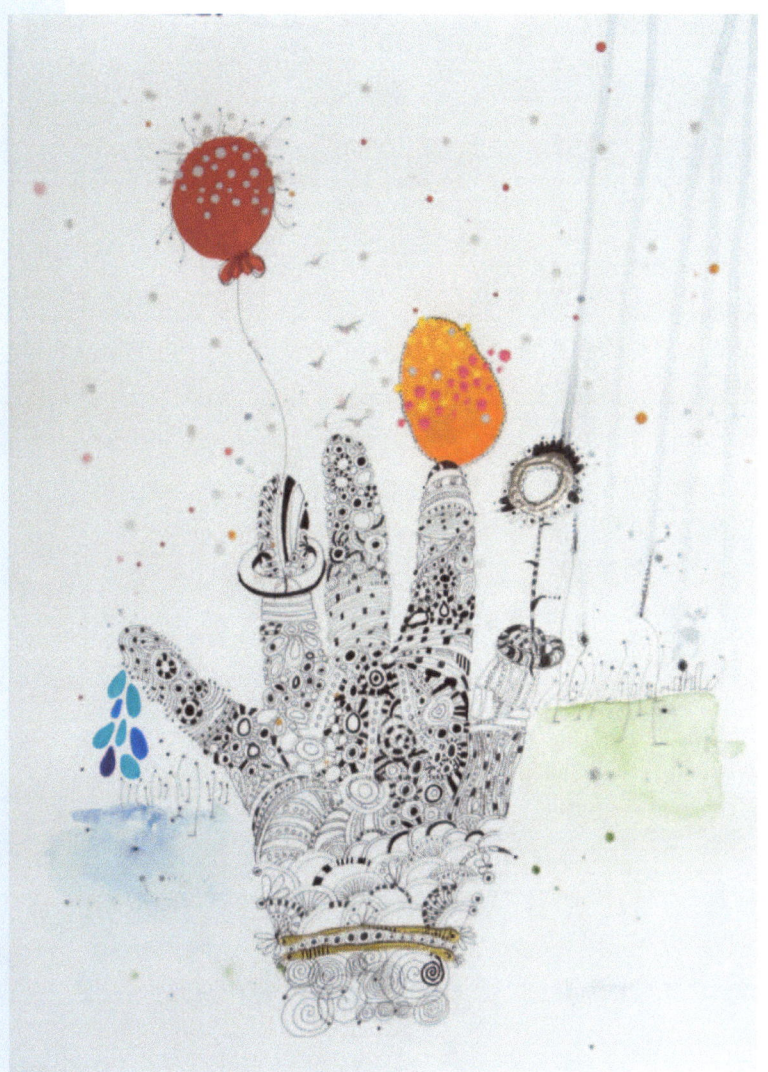

Title: Hand Story
Size: 15" x 11"
Medium: oil, acrylic, ink, watercolor on arches
Date: 2014

Karrie Ross : LA Artcore Union Center for the Arts 2014

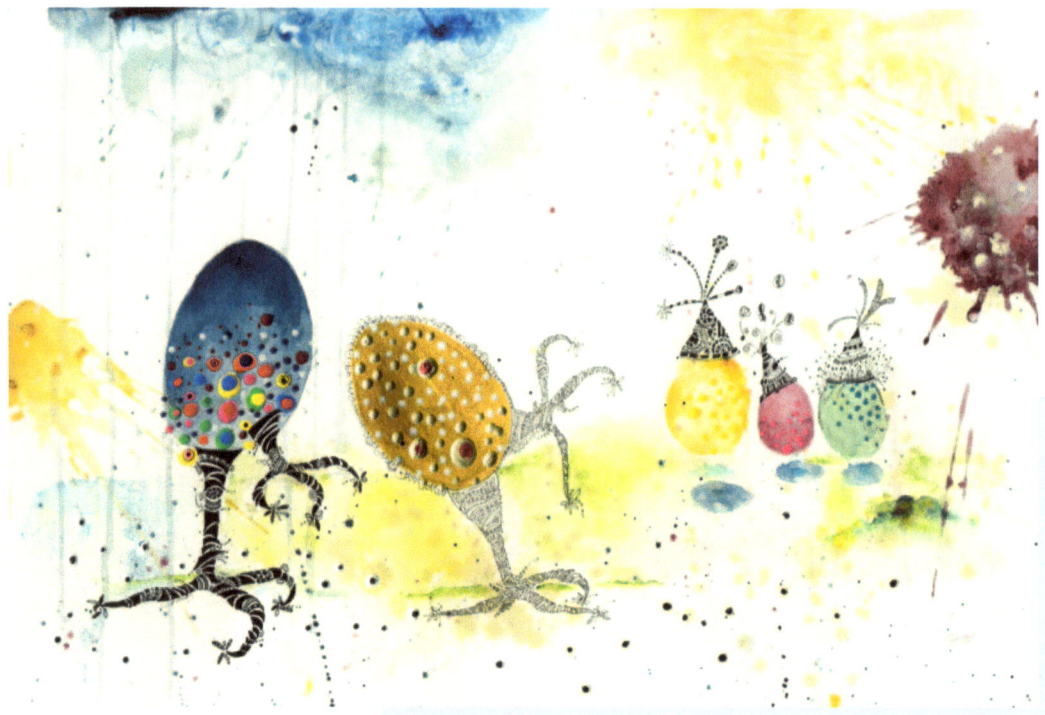

Title: Party!
Size: 15" x 22"
Medium: oil, acrylic, ink, watercolor on arches
Date: 2013

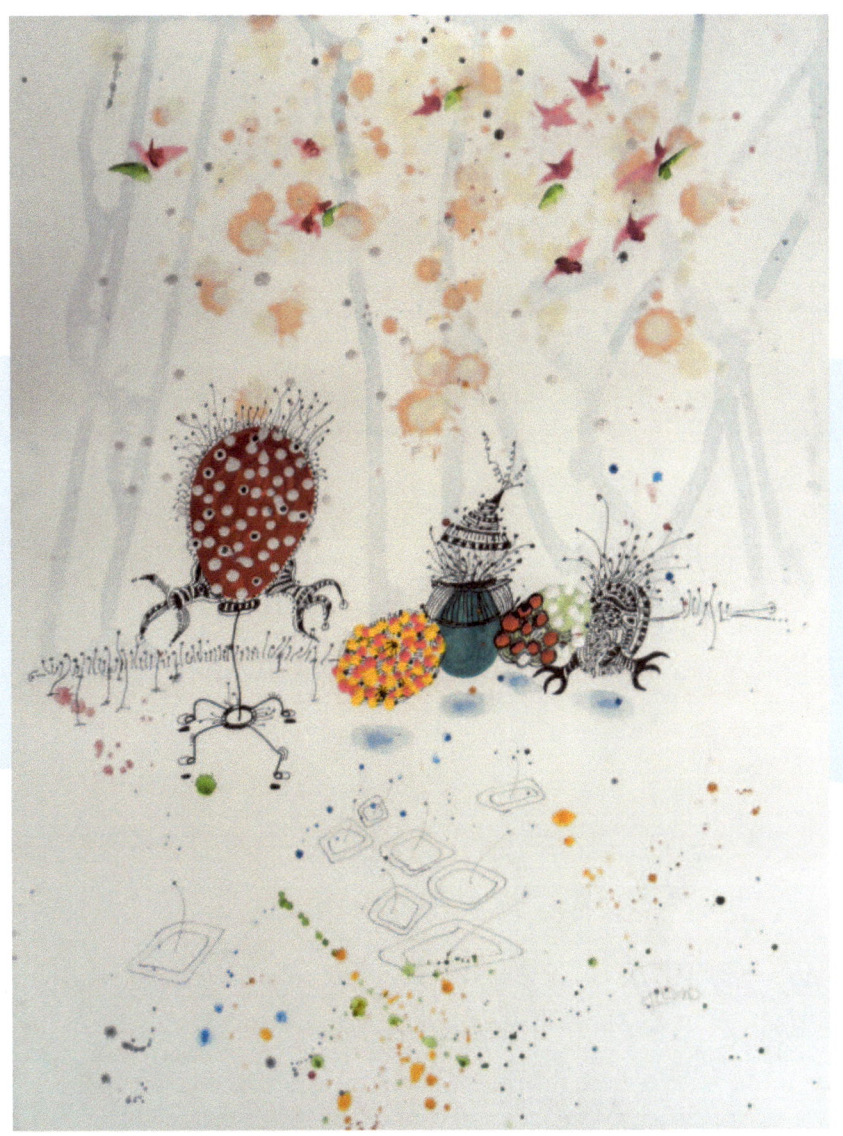

Title: Party Time Class
Size: 15" x 11"
Medium: oil, acrylic, ink, watercolor on arches
Date: 2014

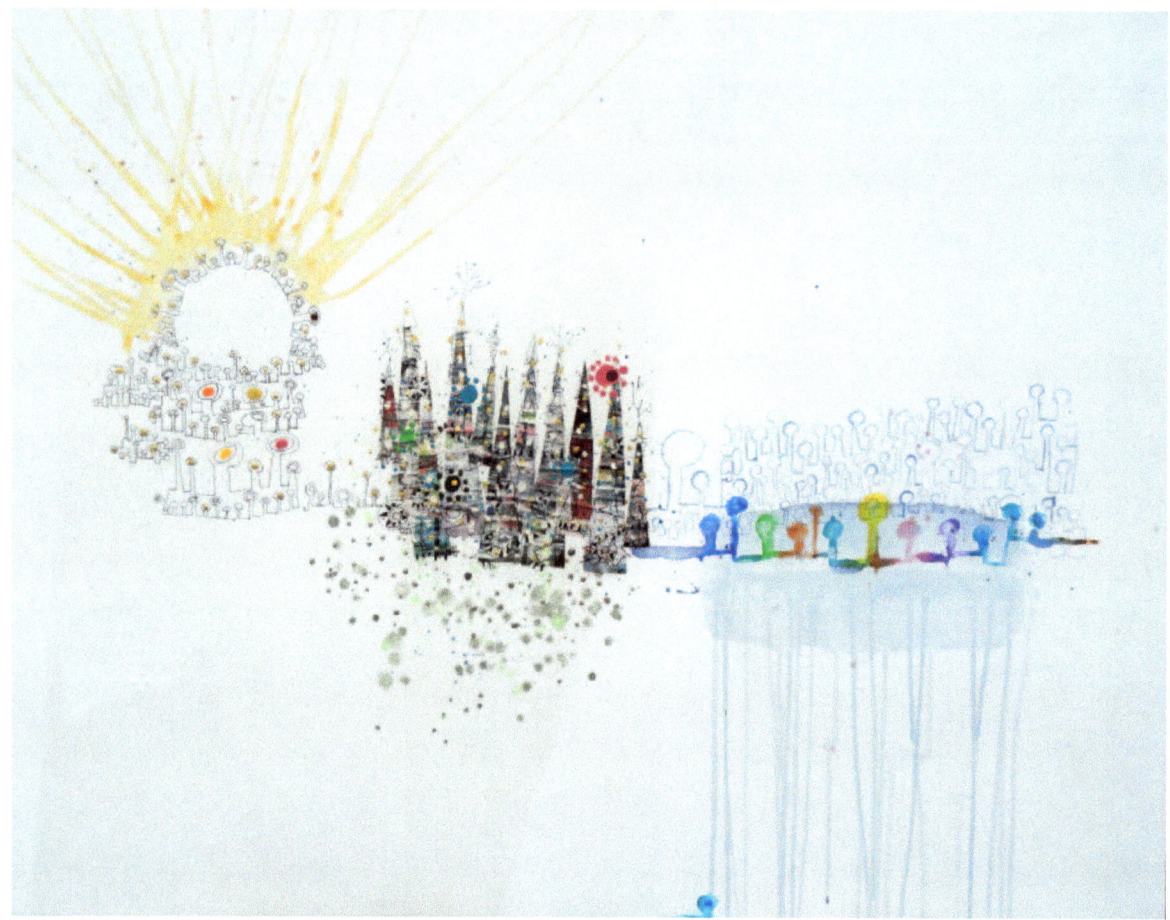

Title: California Dreaming from the Desert to the Sea
Size: 36" x 48"
Medium: oil, acrylic, ink, collage, watercolor on canvas
Date: 2014

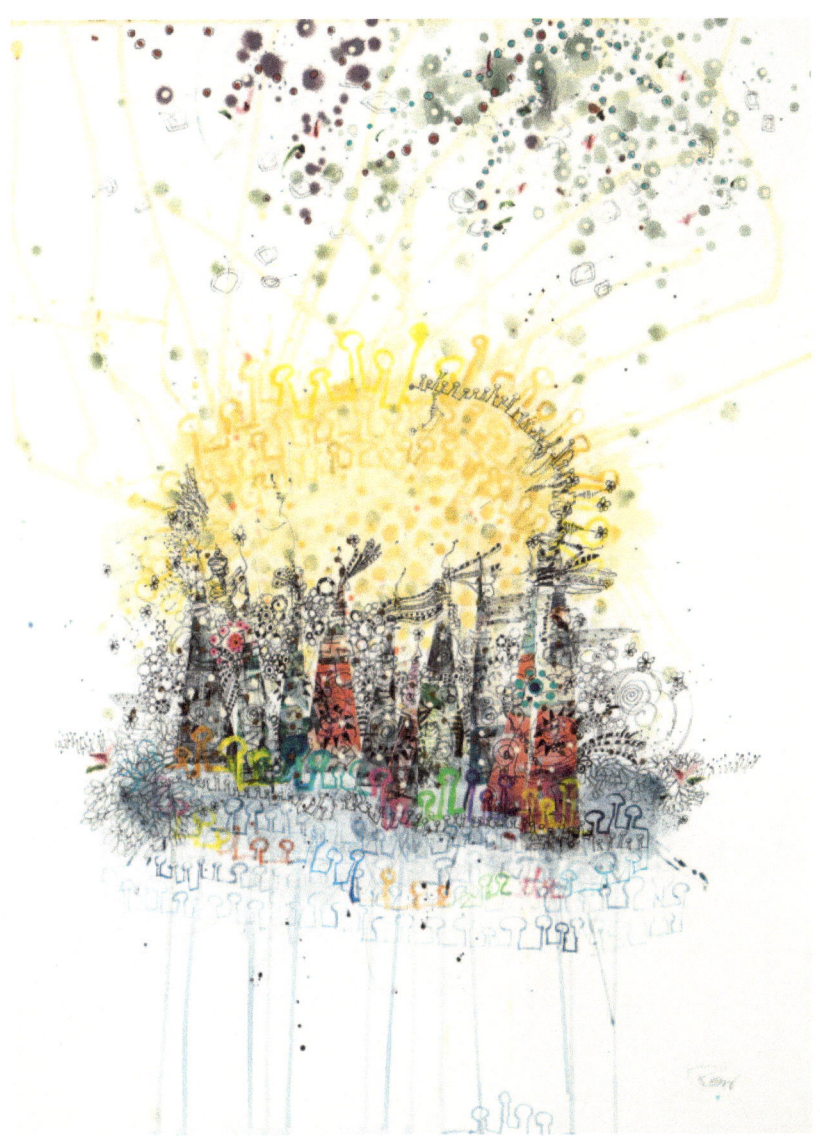

Title: Big Small California Dreaming
Size: 30" x 22"
Medium: oil, acrylic, ink, collage, watercolor on arches
Date: 2014

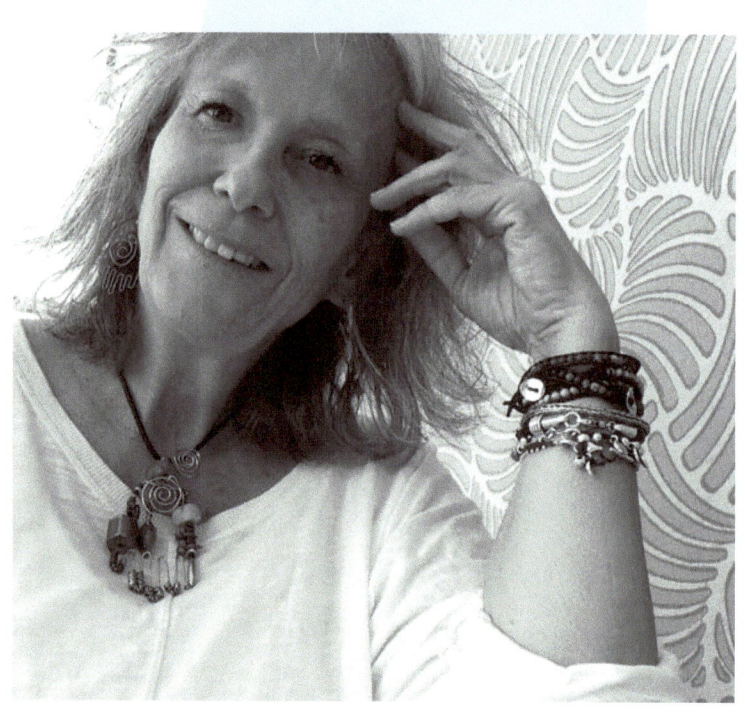

Karrie Ross : LA Artcore Union Center for the Arts 2014

Biography

Karrie Ross, visual Artist.

A native to Los Angeles, California, Karrie Ross was exposed to a vast range of experiences throughout her life. Her parents appreciated ART of all kinds and her childhood was rich in many ways from learning what creative balance was to how to use power tools. Karrie is a survivor. She learned to take care of herself at an early age and has been doing so for most of her life. Her art comes out of her struggles and joys of living. You might see a whimsy on the outside but on the inside there are the everyday things we all experience. Fears, insecurities along with the normal wants and needs of day-to-day living and making ends meet. Karrie's art is her way to manage the bombardment of all this… when asked "What would she do if she didn't have it?" she shook her head and responded, "I wouldn't want to try."

Karrie's art started being shown around Los Angeles in the 1980s, her purpose was to be seen, learn to talk about her art and create a collectors base. She works in both watercolor and oil as they seem "more alive" and pen & ink or pencil for her never-ending fascination with doodling.

Professional sales began in the 1990s, being represented by a High-Point Gallery that worked with the decorative industry and for the next 12 years her paintings were found hanging on the walls of hotels in Japan and New York, and commercial, residential, and retail venues such as: IDA, Macy's, FAO Schwartz, MayCo., Dillards, Sax Fifth Ave, Gladmans, Coach, JCPenney's, Khol's, FredMyers, AGI, Hirshbedner, etc. as well as displayed in high-end interior design showrooms like Baker Design at the PDC. On-air exposure: TV and cable shows CSI Miami, The Standoff, Entourage, Medium; Movies: Shadowboxer, Burn After Reading to name a few. Karrie's artwork can be found in private and corporate local, national, and international collections.

Ross' art has been featured at: the Lancaster Museum MOAH, the Brand Library, the Annual International "Ink and Clay" exhibition at the Kellogg University Art Gallery, Pomona; LA Artcore Union Center for the arts; three Museum location traveling show 2014-2015, to the grand Salone d'Ingresso of Il Palazzo della Provincia di Frosinone, Italy and at the OMA Oceanside Museum of Art and RAM Riverside Art Museum in California; the Los Angeles Municipal Arts Gallery; and interviewed by two Arts Entertainment shows, as well as exhibitions at galleries local and regional. Artslant.com, the #1 Contemporary Artist Network website,

Karrie Ross : LA Artcore Union Center for the Arts 2014

has spotlighted her work among first round Showcase winners for both painting and mixed media. She was a member of the Los Angeles Art Association, Gallery 825, for over 5yrs.

PUBLICATION: Her art and exhibitions have been written about in Cartwheel, Thrillist/LA, Hollywood Today, Topanga Messenger, Santa Monica SUN, American Chronicle, Santa Monica Mirror, the Examiner, the Los Angeles Times, the Huffington Post, to name a few.

AWARDS: Spiral Series: Energy Bloom subset have won honorable mentions in two juried art award shows and one for the Blossoms II National show. The "Portraits" series, the head of "Freedom" won an honorable mention in the 2012 Whole9 Traveling Peace Project. And "As the Cloud Weeps: Bejeweled Bird" won 3rd place in a local show in 2013. She is also an award-winning author of a non-fiction book and childrens picture book.

KARRIE runs an award winning graphic design business (over 25 years) that specializes in the design of fiction and non-fiction books, and collateral for self publishing authors, services, products and small businesses. She consults on brand recognition, marketing, merchandising, and on how to create a web-presence. She served on the Board of Directors for the Art Directors Club of Los Angeles for 5 years in the 1980s.

In the end, Ross is about the seeing of oneself and the knowing of ones personal energy.

Her work is her on going creative exploration.

Karrie Ross : LA Artcore Union Center for the Arts 2014

Solo Exhibitions

2014 LA Artcore Union Center for the Arts; Three Artists; Los Angeles, CA
2014 Sundance Cinema Art Gallery, West Hollywood; Spiral Series; West Hollywood, CA
2013 AlteredSpace Gallery: "Patterns"; Abbot Kinney, Three Artists. Curated by Bryan Chagoll, Venice Beach, CA
2006 KTGY Group, Inc. 4 month office installation, Orange County, CA
2003-2005 Boritzer/Gray/Hamano Gallery; Bergamot Station: Santa Monica, CA

Select Museum/College/NonProfit Exhibitions

– Traveling International Show (2014-2015) "California Dreaming" An International Portrait of Southern California, Jurors: Alfio Borghese, Gallery Director of Il Palazzo della Provincia di Frosinone, Peter Frank. The exhibition will be seen at the following venues:

- Palazzo della Provincia di Frosinone, Frosinone, Italy
- Oceanside Museum of Art, OMA, Oceanside CA
- Riverside Art Museum, RAM, Riverside, CA

– Kellogg University Art Gallery: "INK & CLAY"; Jurors: Jeannie Denhol, Dave Lefner, Phyllis Green, Pamona, CA
– MOAH Museum of Art History Lancaster: "National Treasure California Poppy"; Curated by Andi Campognone; Lancaster, CA
– The Brand Library – "Works on Paper #25, #30 and #42"; Juror for #42: Jack Rutberg, Glendale, CA
– Los Angeles Municipal Gallery, Barnsdale Park; Los Angeles
– Century Gallery: "Symbols/Signs", Northridge, CA

Art Fairs

– World Wide Art Fair, LA Convention Center, Art Unified, Los Angeles, CA
– LA Art Show: LA Convention Center; Fabrik; Los Angeles, CA

Select Gallery Group Exhibitions

2014
– Porch Gallery: Venice Institute of Contemporary Arts; "Water Works": Traveling show. Curated by Juri Koll, Ojai, CA
– Studio C Gallery: Santa Fe Arts Colony: "Oneira: I Dream the Self"; Juror: Betty Brown; Los Angeles, CA
– Install: "Our Ever Changing World: Through the Eyes of Artists": One night event. Question: "What are you saving from extinction?"; Book Signing and Art Exhibit; group showing of all 36 artists in the book; Los Angeles, CA
– Topanga Canyon Gallery; Annual Show; AWARD Third Place; Juror: Jim Morphesis. Topanga, CA

2013
– Bleicher/Golightly/Gorman: "From Little Things Big Things Grow"; Santa Monica, CA
– Broadway Art Space:Group Show: "Women Make the World Go Round"; Santa Monica, CA
– The Peace Project 2013; Whole-9; one of 165 pieces that will be reproduced as 1'x1' squares for a traveling show. Culver City, CA
– Red Pipe Gallery: "City & Self"; Curated by Mat Gleason; Los Angeles, CA
– Garboushian Gallery: "MANA" Fundraiser: Curated by Lori Garboushian; Beverly Hills, CA

2012
– The Peace Project 2012; Honorable mention; Whole-9; Traveline Show, Culver City, CA

– LAX, Terminal One: "Le Petite Jardin"; Los Angeles, CA – 6mons install
– Billboard Art in two Cities: Reading, PA, and Corona, CA

2011
– Chicago Billboard Project: Ten images with the words, "Breast Awareness" . Chicago, Ill
– Pacific Art League: National Competition, Juror: JoAnne Northrup, San Jose Museum of Art, Palo Alto, CA
– Gallery 825: Annual Auction; "Oh The Two Of Us" SOLD to Mr. and Mrs. Herair Garboushian; Los Angeles, CA
– Shoshana Wayne Gallery: "Chain Letter" curated by Christian Cummings & Doug Harvey; over 1,700 artists participated—it was truly an ART Happening; Santa Monica, CA
– Gallery 825: "Not A Car"; Jurors: Silvia Sonnenschmidt and Thomas Volkmann; Los Angeles, CA

2010
– Blossoms II Award Show: AWARD: Honorable Mention awarded to Spiral Series: Energy Blooms: "We Dance"; selected from 2,300 entries; Susan Kathleen Black Foundation
– Williams-Sonoma Home; Fall Wall Decor: "Graffiti"
– TAG Gallery, "California Open" Bergamot Station; Juror: Karen Moss; Santa Monica, CA
– Santa Monica Cultural Affairs; Annenberg Beach House; Santa Monica, CA
– The Brewery Art Walk; Los Angeles, CA

1999-2008 Selected sales to the decorative industry through a gallery at High Point, Atlanta, GA
2009 The Brewery Art Walk, Los Angeles, CA
2001 United Way: 'The Pier' on permanent display at corporate offices Los Angeles, CA

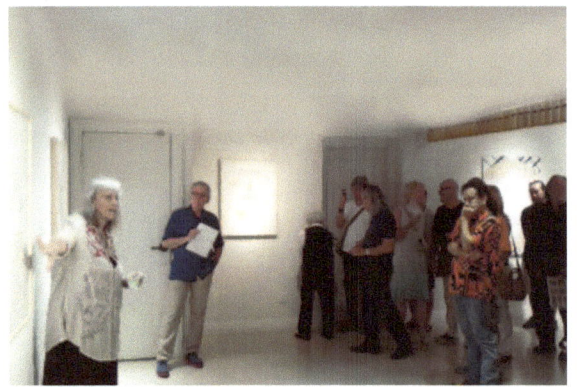
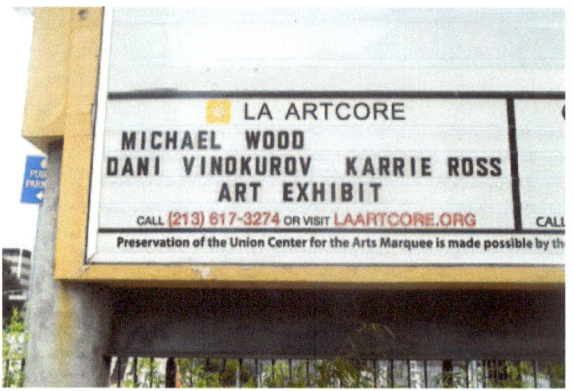
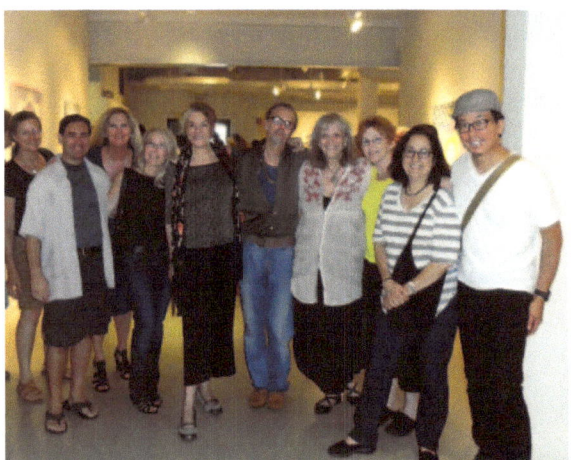
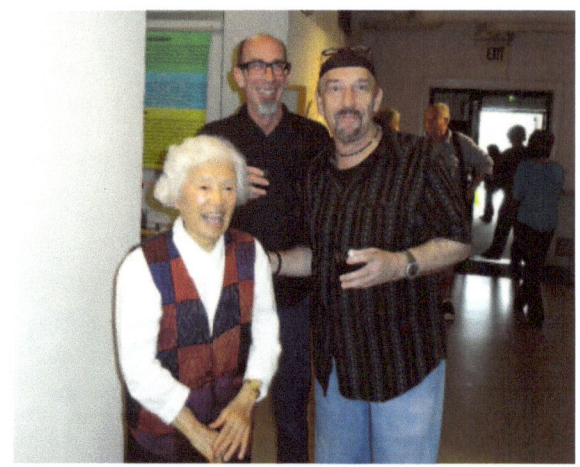
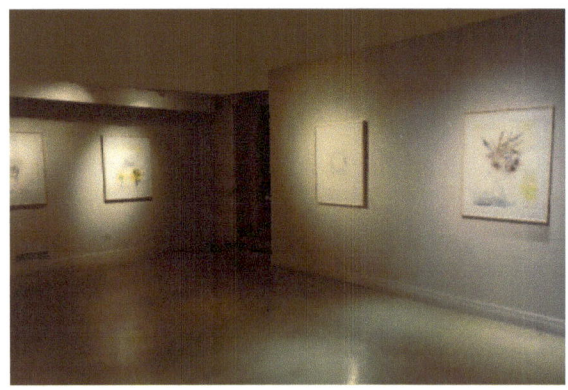
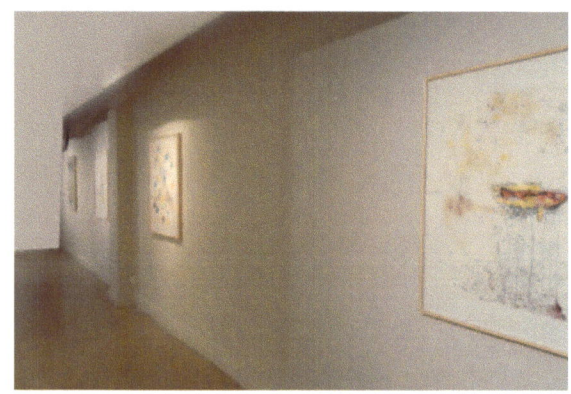

Karrie Ross : LA Artcore Union Center for the Arts 2014

www.ingramcontent.com/pod-product-compliance
Lightning Source LLC
Chambersburg PA
CBHW050907180526
45159CB00007B/2814